Orangutans

ABDO
Publishing Company

A Buddy Book
by
Julie Murray

VISIT US AT
www.abdopub.com

Published by Buddy Books, an imprint of ABDO Publishing Company, 4940 Viking Drive, Suite 622, Edina, Minnesota 55435. Copyright © 2005 by Abdo Consulting Group, Inc. International copyrights reserved in all countries. No part of this book may be reproduced in any form without written permission from the publisher.

Printed in the United States.

Edited by: Christy DeVillier
Contributing Editors: Matt Ray, Michael P. Goecke
Graphic Design: Maria Hosley
Image Research: Deborah Coldiron
Photographs: Corbis, DigitalVision, Minden Pictures, Photodisc

Library of Congress Cataloging-in-Publication Data

Murray, Julie, 1969-
   Orangutans/Julie Murray.
       p. cm. — (Animal kingdom. Set II)
   Includes bibliographical references (p.).
   Contents: Great apes—Orangutans—Size and color—Their bodies—Where they live—Getting around—Food—Living alone—Babies.
   ISBN 1-59197-327-9
       1. Orangutan—Juvenile literature. [1. Orangutan.] I. Title.

QL737.P96M8735 2003
599.88'3—dc21

2003044317

Contents

Great Apes

What do orangutans, chimpanzees, gorillas, and bonobos have in common? All of these animals are great apes. Great apes are bigger than monkeys and lemurs. They do not have tails.

Orangutan

Chimpanzee

Bonobo

Gorilla

Great apes belong to a group called **primates**. Primates have eyes that look forward. Most have flat nails instead of claws. Many primates can grab and hold things. Monkeys, lemurs, baboons, and people are primates, too.

Lemur

Monkey

Baboon

Orangutans

Orang and *utan* are Malay words. Orangutan means "person of the forest." As **primates**, orangutans are like people in some ways. Primates can use tools. They have **communication** skills. Primates are some of the smartest animals.

What They Look Like

Orangutans are big animals. They grow to become between four and five feet (one and two m) tall. Male adults may weigh as much as 200 pounds (91 kg). Females are much smaller. They may weigh as much as 120 pounds (54 kg).

An orangutan grows to become as heavy as a person.

Some people call orangutans "red apes." They have shaggy, red hair. Parts of their face, hands, and feet are hairless. Some orangutans grow beards. Male adults have cheek pads and a throat pouch.

This adult orangutan has large cheek pads.

Orangutans grab branches with their hands and feet as they move through the trees.

Orangutans have long, strong arms. Their legs are shorter. They have five fingers on each hand. They have five toes on each foot. Orangutans can grab things with their hands and feet. This helps them move from tree to tree.

Where They Live

There are two main groups of orangutans. One group is the Sumatran orangutans. They live on the island of Sumatra. The other group is the Bornean orangutans. They live on the island of Borneo. Sumatra and Borneo are islands in Indonesia.

Map of Southeast Asia

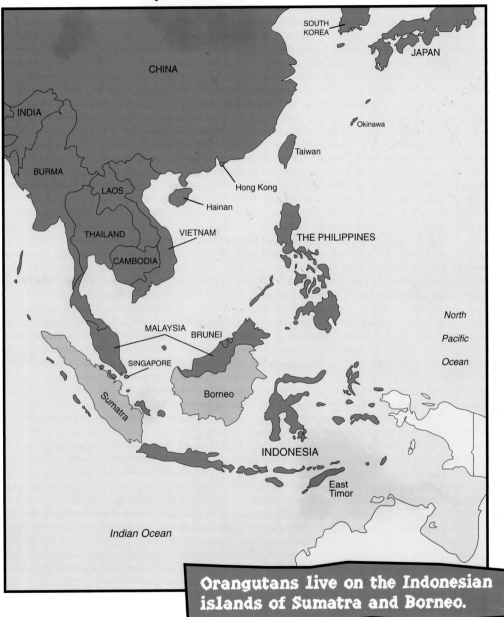

SOUTH KOREA

JAPAN

CHINA

INDIA

Okinawa

Taiwan

BURMA

LAOS

Hong Kong

Hainan

THAILAND

VIETNAM

THE PHILIPPINES

CAMBODIA

North

MALAYSIA

BRUNEI

Pacific

SINGAPORE

Ocean

Sumatra

Borneo

INDONESIA

East
Timor

Indian Ocean

Orangutans live on the Indonesian islands of Sumatra and Borneo.

Orangutans live in rain forests.

Orangutans spend most of their time in the trees. They are the largest **arboreal** animals. Orangutans live in **tropical** rain forests. They travel by swinging from tree branch to tree branch.

On the ground, orangutans use their arms and legs to walk. They can stand up and walk on two legs, too. But they do not walk this way very often.

Orangutan Life

Orangutans do not live in large groups like other **primates**. They live alone most of the time. Mating orangutans spend a few days together. Mother orangutans live with their young as long as seven years.

Orangutan mothers stay close to their young.

Orangutans eat and sleep in the trees. They build nests from tree branches and leaves. Orangutans rest, play, and sleep in their nests. They may make a new nest every day.

Eating

Orangutans spend their time searching for food. They eat leaves, bark, flowers, nuts, seeds, eggs, and vegetables. Orangutans eat a lot of fruit, too. They enjoy figs, mangoes, bananas, and plums. Orangutans remember which fruit trees they have visited. They go back to the same trees every year to eat the ripe fruit.

This orangutan is eating bananas.

Some fruits are hard to eat. They are covered with sharp hairs that cut. Some orangutans use a tool to eat these prickly fruits. They use a stick to crack open the fruit. Then, they eat the fruit's seeds without touching the sharp hairs.

Baby Orangutans

Female orangutans can have babies about every four years. They commonly have one baby at a time. A newborn orangutan weighs between two and four pounds (one and two kg). It holds on to its mother's underside.

Baby orangutans cling to their mother's underside.

Baby orangutans drink their mother's milk. After about four months, they begin eating other foods. After one year, the young orangutans ride on their mother's back. They watch their mother and learn from her. In time, young orangutans learn how to find their own food.

Female orangutans become adults after about nine years. Males become adults around the age of 14. Adult orangutans live on their own. They may live as long as 40 years in the wild.

Orangutan Facts

- Orangutans are friendly animals.

- An orangutan is six times stronger than a person is.

- Leopards and tigers are animals that hunt orangutans.

- Orangutans use their big toes like thumbs.

- Long ago, orangutans lived throughout much of Southeast Asia.

- Today orangutans are in danger of dying out.

Important Words

arboreal describes animals that spend most of their lives in trees.

communication giving and receiving information.

primate a group that people, apes, and monkeys belong to.

tropical weather that is warm and wet.

Web Sites

To learn more about orangutans, visit ABDO Publishing Company on the World Wide Web. Web sites about orangutans are featured on our Book Links page. These links are routinely monitored and updated to provide the most current information available.

www.abdopub.com

Index